Song
OF
Songs

THE
PASSION
TRANSLATION

Song OF Songs

DIVINE
ROMANCE

Translated from Hebrew and Greek Texts

DR. BRIAN SIMMONS

tPt
BIBLE

BroadStreet
PUBLISHING

Song of Songs: Divine Romance, The Passion Translation®
Translated from the original Hebrew and Greek texts by Dr. Brian Simmons

Published by BroadStreet Publishing Group, LLC
Racine, Wisconsin, USA
www.broadstreetpublishing.com

© 2014 The Passion Translation®

ISBN-13: 9781424549573 (paperback)
ISBN-13: 9781424549771 (e-book)

Cover and interior design by Garborg Design Works, Inc. | www.garborgdesign.com
Interior typesetting by Katherine Lloyd | www.theDESKonline.com

Printed in the United States of America

Translator's Introduction

Allow me to explain a few things about The Passion Translation. To translate God's Word from Hebrew and Greek into another language is both a difficult task and a delightful one. The Passion Translation has been a project I've wanted to give myself to for many years. And recently it seemed the Lord spoke deeply into my heart that he wanted me to make this project a reality. So I have begun with my favorite book in the Bible, the Song of Solomon, also known as the Song of Songs.

I have fallen in love with this sweetest song of all the ages. We see the Shulamite's breathtaking and beautiful journey unveiled in this anointed allegory. It is the path every passionate lover will choose. But this divine parable penned by Solomon also describes the journey that every longing lover of Jesus will find as his or her very own.

So why another translation? Many wonderful versions of the Bible now grace our bookshelves, bookstores, software programs, even applications on our phones. So why add one more? The reason is simple: God wants his message of love to be received in every culture, community, and language. So what about the language of love? The language of the heart best expresses the passion of this love theology. That is the purpose of The Passion Translation.

By translating this portion of the Word of God, the Song of Songs, I have attempted to translate not only from a scholarly or linguistic perspective but from the passion of a heart on fire. Love will always find a language to express itself. Fiery love for Jesus pushes our thoughts out of hiding and puts them into anointed words of adoration. This articulation, out of the deepest places of our hearts, moves God and inspires each of us to a greater devotion. Everyone deserves to hear and feel the passion of our Bridegroom for his radiant and soon-to-be-perfected bride.

The inspired Song of Songs is a work of art. It is a melody sung from the heart of Jesus Christ for his longing bride. It is full of symbols, subtle art forms, poetry, and nuances that the translator must convey in order to bring it forth adequately to the English reader. This is what I have attempted to do with this project. Some of the cultural symbols that conveyed rich texture of meaning to the Hebrew speaker nearly three thousand years ago have become almost impossible to leave in their literal form, since the English speaker of today has little or no connection to those symbols. This requires that much of the hidden meanings locked into the Hebrew text be made explicit. That is why I have chosen to make this a dynamic equivalent of transferring the meaning, not just the words, into a form that many will find refreshing.

Moreover, in reading this Shulamite's journey, the story line is often missed or overlooked. I believe the Holy Spirit has hidden within the Song of Songs an amazing story—a story of how Jesus makes his bride beautiful and holy by casting out her fear with perfect love. This sent-from-heaven revelation is waiting to be received with all its intensity and power to unlock the deepest places of our hearts.

Unfortunately, for some, the Song of Songs has become merely a book expressing sexuality, with hidden meanings and symbols of sensuality. Many modern expositors teach from the Song of Songs the sexual relationship appropriate to a husband and wife. They find it difficult when others see the symbols and apply them to the spiritual journey every believer must take as we move further into the passionate heart of our heavenly Bridegroom. Their fear is that we "over spiritualize" the Song of Songs. How hard that would be! How wonderfully spiritual and holy is this song of all songs!

Every symbol the reader encounters must be seen as a form of "virtual reality" that can, when properly interpreted, help us in our pursuit of Jesus Christ until we are fully his. Truly, if this is the song of all songs, its theme goes beyond and reaches higher than mere human sexuality.

So be prepared to see yourself in this journey and to hear his lyrics of love sung over you. Invest the time to read this through in one sitting. Then go back and read slowly and carefully, pondering each verse and praying through each love principle revealed in this translation. I think you may be shocked to read some of the things spoken over your life, considering them almost too good to be true. May heaven's glorious Bridegroom, the Beloved of your soul, come and manifest himself to you in a wonderful and breathtaking fashion as you read Song of Songs in *The Passion Translation*. My prayer is that you will be as thrilled with what you read as I have been in translating it.

This book is dedicated to every passionate lover of Jesus. May the Holy Spirit take you by the hand and lead you out in pursuit of your Beloved.

—Dr. Brian Simmons

One

———

¹The most amazing song of all, by King Solomon.

[The Shulamite][a]

²Smother me with kisses—
Your Spirit kiss divine.[b]
So kind are your caresses,[c]
I drink them in
Like the sweetest wine![d]

---

a 1:2 The word for *Shulamite* and the word for *Solomon* are taken from the same Hebrew root word; one masculine, the other feminine. We are one spirit with our King, united with him. You have become the Shulamite.

b 1:2 This Spirit kiss is what made Adam, the man of clay, into a living expression of God. Dust and Deity met when the Maker kissed his Spirit wind into Adam. The Word of God is the kiss from the mouth of our Beloved, breathing upon us the revelation of his love.

c 1:2 Or "your breasts" or "your loves." The Hebrew text literally means "your loves." This speaks of his saving love, keeping love, forgiving love, and embracing love. The love of Jesus cannot be singular; it is so infinite it must be described in the plural.

d 1:4 There is a wordplay in the Hebrew, similar to a pun. The word for "kisses" and the word for "take a drink (wine)," is nearly the same. The implication, as seen by ancient expositors, is that God's lovers will be drunk with love, the intoxicating kisses of his mouth. The Hebrew word for "kiss" is *nashaq*, which can also mean "to equip" or "to arm (for battle)." We need his kisses to become equipped warriors for him.

³Your presence releases
A fragrance so pleasing—
Over and over poured out.
For your lovely name is "Flowing Oil."
No wonder the brides-to-be adore you.
⁴Draw me into your heart and lead me out.
We will run away together—
Into your cloud-filled chamber.ᵃ

[The Chorus of Friends]

We will remember your love
As we laugh and rejoice in you,
Celebrating your every kiss
As better than wine.
No wonder righteousness
Adores you!

[The Shulamite]

⁵Jerusalem maidens,
In this twilight darkness,ᵇ
I know I am so unworthy—so in need.

---

a 1:4 The Hebrew text literally means "a chamber inside a chamber." This points us to the Holy of Holies inside the temple chamber.

b 1:5 Or "black." The Hebrew root word used here for "black" or "dark" means "twilight darkness" or "morning gray."

[The Shepherd-King]

Yet you are so lovely!

[The Shulamite]

I feel as dark and dry as the desert tents
Of the wandering nomads.[a]

[The Shepherd-King]

Yet you are so lovely—
Like the fine linen tapestry
Hanging in the Holy Place.

[The Shulamite to her friends]

[6]Please don't stare in scorn
Because of my dark and sinful ways.[b]
My angry brothers quarreled with me
And appointed me guardian
Of their ministry vineyards,
Yet I've not guarded my vineyard within.
[7]Won't you tell me, Lover of my soul,

---

a 1:5 Literally, "dark as the tent curtains of Kedar." There is a wordplay in the Hebrew, as the word
   Kedar means "a dark one" or "a dark place." This was the name of one of the sons of Ishmael and
   represents our old Adam life.

b 1:6 The Hebrew text literally means "Many morning suns have darkened me."

Where do you feed your flock?
Where do you lead your beloved ones[a]
To rest in the heat of the day?
For I wish to be wrapped all around you[b]
As I go among the flocks of
Your under-shepherds.
It is you I long for, with no veil between us!

[The Shepherd-King]

[8]Listen, my radiant one.
If you ever lose sight of me,
Just follow in my footsteps
Where I lead my lovers.
Come with your burdens and cares.[c]
Come to the place near
The sanctuary of my shepherds—
There you will find me.
[9]My dearest one,
Let me tell you how I see you—
You are so thrilling to me.
To gaze upon you is like looking
At one of Pharaoh's finest horses—

a   1:7 She sees her Beloved as a shepherd. This is a metaphor of the role he takes in her eyes. We need
    not develop a literal story line of a lover and a shepherd., but a representation of the relationship
    between you and your Beloved, which cannot be described by one symbol or role.

b   1:7 Translated from the Septuagint.

c   1:8 Or "graze your goats." This is a metaphor that speaks of her responsibilities and labors.

A strong, regal steed
Pulling his royal chariot.
[10]Your tender cheeks are aglow—
Your earrings and gem-laden necklaces
Set them ablaze.
[11]We will enhance your beauty,[a]
Encircling you
With our golden reins of love.
You will be marked
With our redeeming grace.[b]

[The Shulamite]

[12]As the King surrounded me,
The sweet fragrance of my praise perfume[c]
Awakened the night.
[13]A sachet of myrrh is my Lover,
Like a tied-up bundle of myrrh[d]
Resting over my heart.
[14]He is like a bouquet of henna blossoms—
Henna plucked near the vines

---

a 1:11 This is the Trinity ("We"), which will be involved in making every Shulamite holy and radiant.

b 1:11 The Hebrew text literally means "inlaid with silver." The concept of silver in the Bible always points to redemption, the price paid to set us free.

c 1:12 Or "spikenard."

d 1:13 This bundle of tied-up myrrh is an incredible picture of the cross. Myrrh, known as an embalming spice, is always associated with suffering. The suffering love of Jesus will be over her heart for the rest of her days—the revelation of our Beloved tied onto the cross like a bundle of myrrh.

At the fountain of the Lamb.[a]
I will hold him and never let him part.

[The Shepherd-King]

[15]**Look at you, my dearest darling,**
You are so lovely!
You are beauty itself to me.
Your passionate eyes
Are like loyal, gentle doves.[b]

[The Shulamite]

[16]My Beloved One,
You are pleasing beyond words,
And so winsome!
Our resting place is anointed and flourishing,
Like a green forest meadow bathed in light.
[17]Rafters of cedar branches are over our heads
And balconies of pleasant-smelling pines.
A perfect home!

---

a 1:14 Or, "At Engedi." *Engedi* means "fountain of the Lamb." The Hebrew word for "henna" is a homonym that can mean "atonement" or "redeeming grace."

b 1:15 The Hebrew text literally means "Your eyes are doves." Some see this as a hypocorism, but the dove points us to the Holy Spirit. She is commended for seeing him with spiritual revelation as she perceives the glory of the cross with its "myrrh."

Two

———

¹I am truly his rose,
The very theme of his song.[a]
I am overshadowed by his love,
Growing in the valley.

[The Shepherd-King]

²Yes, you are my darling companion.
You stand out from all the rest.
For though the curse of sin surrounds you,[b]
Still you remain as pure as a lily,[c]
Even more than all others.

---

a 2:1 The Hebrew text says, "a rose of Sharon." The word *Sharon* can be translated "his song." She now sees herself as the one he sings over. The root word for "rose" (Hebrew *habab*) can mean "overshadowed."

b 2:2 This is a thorn bush, which speaks of the curse of sin. See Genesis 3:18, John 19:5, and Galatians 3:13. On the cross, Jesus wore a crown of thorns, for he took away the curse of sin.

c 2:2 The emblem of a lily was engraved on the upper part of the pillars of Solomon's temple. Lilies are symbols of purity in the "temple" of our inner being.

[The Shulamite]

> [3] My Beloved is to me
> The most fragrant apple tree—
> He stands above the sons of men.[a]
> Sitting under his grace shadow,
> I blossom in his shade,
> Enjoying the sweet taste
> Of his pleasant, delicious fruit,
> Resting with delight
> Where his glory never fades.
> [4] Suddenly, he transported me
> Into his house of wine—
> He looked upon me
> With his unrelenting love divine.[b]
> [5] Revive me with your goblet of wine.
> Refresh me again with your sweet promises.
> Help me and hold me, for I am lovesick![c]
> I am longing for more—
> Yet how could I take more?[d]
> [6] His left hand cradles my head

---

a 2:3 Or "trees of the forest." Trees in the Bible are often metaphors for humanity.

b 2:4 Or "His banner covering me was love."

c 2:5 Or "wounded by love."

d 2:5 Implied in the context.

While his right hand holds me close.[a]
I am at rest in this love.

[The Shepherd-King]

[7]Promise me, brides-to-be,
By the gentle gazelles[b]
And delicate deer,
That you will not disturb my love
Until she is ready to arise.

[The Shulamite]

[8]Listen! I hear my Lover's voice.
I know it's him coming to me—
Leaping with joy over mountains,
Skipping in love
Over the hills that separate us,[c]
To come to me.
[9]Let me describe him:
He is graceful as a gazelle—
Swift as a wild stag.

---

a 2:6 For more on the right hand and left hand, see Proverbs 3:16.
b 2:7 In the poetic imagery of the Song of Songs, deer and gazelle are symbols of the joys of love. The Septuagint says, "By all the powers and strengths of the field."
c 2:8 Implied in the context of 2:17.

Now he comes closer,
Even to the places where I hide.
Now he gazes into my soul,
Peering through the portal
As he blossoms within my heart.
[10]The one I love calls to me:

[The Bridegroom-King]

Arise, my dearest.
Hurry, my darling.
Come along with me!
I have come as you have asked
To draw you to my heart and lead you out.
For now is the time, my beautiful one.
[11]The season has changed,
The bondage of your
Barren winter has ended,
And the season of hiding is over and gone.
The rains have soaked the earth[a]
[12]And left it bright with blossoming flowers.
The season for pruning the vines has arrived.[b]
I hear the cooing of doves in our land,[c]

---

a 2:11 The rains speak of the outpouring of the Holy Spirit. She is refreshed and prepared to move out with him.

b 2:12 This is the turtledove, which is heard only at the time of harvest. The turtledove is also an acceptable sacrifice of cleansing in the place of a lamb. The words "our land" show the joint possession of all things that we enjoy through our union with Christ.

Filling the air with songs
To awaken you and guide you forth.
¹³Can you not discern
This new day of destiny
Breaking forth around you?
The early signs of my purposes and plans
Are bursting forth.*a*
The budding vines of new life
Are now blooming everywhere.
The fragrance of flowers whispers,
"There is change in the air."
Arise, my love, my beautiful companion,
And run with me to the higher place.
For now is the time to arise
And come away with me.
¹⁴For you are my dove,
Hidden in the split-open rock.*b*
It was I who took you
And hid you up high
In the secret stairway of the sky.
Let me see your radiant face
And hear your sweet voice.*c*

---

a 2:13 This text is literally translated "The fig tree has sweetened and puts forth its early figs." In the language of allegory, the fig tree is a picture of destiny and purpose. The sign of a fig tree blooming is the sign of an early spring, a new season.

b 2:14 This speaks of the wounded side of Jesus, our Rock where we hide and rest.

c 2:14 The Hebrew text literally means "Your voice is delicious."

How beautiful your eyes of worship
And lovely your voice in prayer.
[15]You must catch the troubling foxes,
Those sly little foxes
That hinder our relationship.[a]
For they raid our budding vineyard of love
To ruin what I've planted within you.
Will you catch them
And remove them for me?
We will do it together.

[The Shulamite]

[16]I know my Lover is mine,
And I have everything in you,
For we delight ourselves in each other.[b]
[17]But until the day springs to life
And the shifting shadows of fear disappear,
Turn around, my Lover, and ascend
To the holy mountains of separation
Without me.[c]

---

a 2:15 These "foxes" are the compromises that are hidden deep in our hearts. These are areas of our
   lives where we have not yet allowed the victory of Christ to shine into. The foxes keep the fruit of his
   Spirit from growing within us.

b 2:16 The Hebrew wording includes the phrase "He browses among the lilies." The Hebrew word for
   "browse" can also mean "to take delight in."

c 2:17 This text literally means "mountains of Bether," the Hebrew word for "separation" or "gap." This
   could be the realm of holiness, being separated to God. Some scholars say Bether was a spiritual
   representation of a mountain of fragrant spices; i.e., the realm of holiness.

Until the new day fully dawns,
Run on ahead like the graceful gazelle
And skip like the young stag
Over the mountains of separation.
Go on ahead to the mountain of spices—
I'll come away another time.[a]

a 2:17 Implied in the text.

Three

—

¹Night after night I am tossing and turning
On my bed of travail.
Why did I let him go from me?
How my heart now aches for him,
But he is nowhere to be found.
²So I must rise in search of him,
Looking throughout the city,[a]
Seeking until I find him.
Even if I have to roam through every street,
Nothing will keep me from my search.
Where is he—my soul's true love?
He is nowhere to be found.
³Then I encountered the overseers
As they circled the city.
So I asked them, "Have you found him—
My heart's true love?"

a 3:2 The city is a picture of the local church, a place with government, order, and overseers. She goes
from church to church, looking for the one she loves.

⁴Just as I moved past them,
I encountered him.
I found the one I adore!
I caught him and fastened myself to him,
Refusing to be feeble in my heart again.
Now I will bring him back to the temple within,
Where I was given new birth—
Into my innermost parts,
The place of my conceiving.

[The Bridegroom-King]

⁵Promise me, O Jerusalem maidens,
By the gentle gazelles and delicate deer,
That you'll not disturb my love
Until she is ready to arise.
[The Voice of the Lord]
⁶Who is this one
Ascending from the wilderness
In the pillar of the glory cloud?
He is fragrant with the anointing oils
Of myrrh and frankincense—ᵃ
More fragrant than all the spices of the merchant.
⁷Look! It is the King's marriage carriage.
The love seat surrounded by sixty champions,

a 3:6 These spices are found in the Bible as ingredients of the sacred anointing oil. Myrrh points to the suffering and death of Christ, while frankincense reveals the fragrance of his perfect life and ministry.

The mightiest of Israel's host,
Are like pillars of protection.
⁸They are angelic warriors standing ready
With swords to defend the King and his fiancée
From every terror of the night.
⁹The King made this mercy seat for himself
Out of the finest wood that will not decay.
¹⁰Pillars of smoke, like silver mist—
A canopy of golden glory dwells above it.
The place where they sit together
Is sprinkled with crimson.
Love and mercy cover this carriage,
Blanketing his tabernacle throne.
The King himself has made it
For those who will become his bride.
¹¹Rise up, Zion maidens, brides-to-be!
Come and feast your eyes on this King
As he passes in procession
On his way to his wedding.
This is the day filled
With overwhelming joy—
The day of his great gladness.

Four

[The Bridegroom-King]

¹Listen, my dearest darling,
You are so beautiful—
You are beauty itself to me!
Your eyes glisten with love,
Like gentle doves behind your veil.
What devotion I see
Each time I gaze upon you.
You are like a sacrifice ready to be offered.[a]
²When I look at you I see that you have
Taken my fruit and tasted my Word.
Your life has become clean and pure,

---

a 4:1 The Hebrew text literally means "Your hair is like a flock of goats streaming down Mount Gilead."
There is great symbolism in this verse. Hair is a symbol of our devotion to Christ. Mount Gilead is
where the sacrificial animals were kept in preparation for temple sacrifices. So a goat coming down
Mount Gilead was a sacrifice ready to be offered.

Like a lamb washed and newly shorn.
You now show grace and balance
With truth on display.
³Your lips are as lovely
As Rahab's scarlet ribbon,[a]
Speaking mercy, speaking grace.
The words of your mouth
Are as refreshing as an oasis.
What pleasure you bring to me!
I see your blushing cheeks
Opened like the halves of a pomegranate,[b]
Showing through your veil
Of tender meekness.
⁴When I look at you
I see your inner strength,
So stately and strong.
You are as secure as David's fortress.
Your virtues and grace
Cause a thousand famous soldiers
To surrender to your beauty.
⁵Your pure faith and love
Rest over your heart

---

a 4:3 The "scarlet ribbon" in the text is a comparison to the ribbon Rahab placed at her dwelling to show the place where mercy would spare her life. The color scarlet points us to the blood of mercy, Christ's sacrifice that has spared us. See Joshua 2.

b 4:3 Pomegranates were engraved on the tops of the pillars of Solomon's temple and were also sewn into the hem of the robes of the high priest. They speak of our open hearts of love, filled with passion for him.

As you nurture those
Who are yet infants.

[The Shulamite]

[6]I've made up my mind.
Until the darkness disappears
And the dawn has fully come,
In spite of shadows and fears,
I will go to the mountaintop with you.
I will climb with you
The mountain of suffering love[a]
And the hill of burning incense.
Yes, I will be your bride.

[The Bridegroom-King]

[7]Every part of you
Is so beautiful, my darling.
Perfect your beauty,
Without flaw within.
[8]Now you are ready, bride of the mountains,
To come with me as we climb
The highest peaks together.

---

a   4:6 Literally, "the mountain of myrrh"—the emblem of suffering love. To become the bride, she must experience Calvary, as did her Lord. We must be his co-crucified partner who will embrace the fellowship of his sufferings. See Galatians 2:20 and Philippians 3:10.

Come with me through the archway of trust.[a]
We will look down
From the crest of the glistening mounts
And from the summit of our sublime sanctuary.
Together we will wage war
In the lion's den and the leopard's lair
As they watch nightly for their prey.
[9]For you reach into my heart.
With one flash of your eyes
I am undone by your love,
My beloved, my equal, my bride.
You leave me breathless—
I am overcome by merely a glance
From your worshipping eyes,
For you have stolen my heart.
I am held hostage by your love
And by the graces of
Righteousness shining upon you.[b]
[10]How satisfying to me,
My equal, my bride.
Your love is my finest wine—
Intoxicating and thrilling.
And your sweet, perfumed praises—
So exotic, so pleasing.

---

a 4:8 Translated from the Septuagint.
b 4:9 Literally, "the ornaments of your neck."

¹¹Your loving words are like the honeycomb to me;
Your tongue releases milk and honey,
For I find the Promised Land
Flowing within you.
The fragrance of your worshipping love
Surrounds you with scented robes of white.
¹²My darling bride, my private paradise,
Fastened to my heart.
A secret spring are you
That no one else can have—
My bubbling fountain
Hidden from public view.
What a perfect partner to me,
Now that I have you.
¹³⁻¹⁴Your inward life is now sprouting,
Bringing forth fruit.
What a beautiful paradise
Unfolds within you.
When I'm near you
I smell aromas of the finest spice,
For many clusters of
My exquisite fruit
Now grow within your inner garden.
Here are nine:
Pomegranates of passion,[a]

---

a 4:13–14 "Pomegranate" is taken from a word that means "exalted." The temple pillars were adorned with pomegranates.

Henna from heaven,[a]
Spikenard so sweet,[b]
Saffron shining,[c]
Fragrant calamus from the cross,[d]
Sacred cinnamon,[e]
Branches of scented woods,[f]
Myrrh, like tears from a tree,[g]
And aloe as eagles ascending.[h]
[15]Your life flows into mine,
Pure as a garden spring.
A well of living water
Springs up from within you,
Like a mountain brook
Flowing into my heart.

---

a 4:13-14 "Henna" comes from a root word for "ransom price" or "redemption." The fruit of mercy is seen in his maturing bride.

b 4:13-14 The Hebrew root word for "spikenard" means "light." She is walking in the light as he is the Light.

c 4:13-14 Saffron is the crocus, the lover's perfume, costly and fragrant.

d 4:13-14 Calamus is taken from a marsh plant known as "sweet flag," which produces fragrant oil. The Hebrew word for this spice means "purchased" or "redeemed."

e 4:13-14 Cinnamon emits a fragrance that is representative of an odor of holiness to the Lord. It was used in the sacred anointing oil of the priests and the tabernacle.

f 4:13-14 This is the incense that would be burned on the golden altar in the Holy Place.

g 4:13-14 Known as "tears from a tree," myrrh was a resin spice formed by cutting a tree. It is a picture of the suffering love of Christ dripping down from Calvary's tree.

h 4:13-14 Aloe is considered by many as a healing balm. The presence of the Lord within her is released as a healing balm to those she touches. Jesus' robes smelled of aloe (Psalm 45:8). One of the names used by some for aloe is "eagle wood." Like eagles, we fly above our wounds, free from the past as we walk in intimacy with him.

[The Shulamite Bride]

4:16-5:1Then may your awakening breath
Blow upon my life until I am fully yours.
Breathe upon me with your Spirit wind.
Stir up the sweet spice of your life within me.
Spare nothing as you make me
Your fruitful garden.
Hold nothing back until I release your fragrance.
Come walk with me as you walked
With Adam in your paradise garden.[a]
Come taste the fruits of your life in me.

[The Bridegroom-King]

**I have come to you, my darling bride,
For you are my paradise garden!**

[The Shulamite Bride]

Come walk with me
Until I am fully yours.
Come taste the fruits
Of your life in me.

---

a 4:16–5:1 The scene of a garden and the breath of God point us back to Eden. Now this paradise is found in his bride. This is the reason the reference of Adam is given: to help the reader connect with the mystery of this scene.

Five

[The Bridegroom-King]

I have gathered from your heart,
My equal, my bride,
I have gathered from my garden
All my sacred spices—even my myrrh.
I have tasted and enjoyed
My wine within you.
I have tasted with pleasure
My pure milk, my honeycomb,
Which you yield to me.
I delight in gathering my sacred spice,
All the fruits of my life that I have
Gathered from within you,
My paradise garden.
Come, all my friends—
Feast upon my bride,

All you revelers of my palace.
Feast on her, my lovers!
Drink and drink, and drink again,
Until you can take no more.
Drink the wine of her love.
Take all you desire, you priests.
My life within her
Will become your feast.[a]

[The Shulamite Bride]

[2]After this I let my devotion slumber,
But my heart for him stayed awake.
I had a dream.
I dreamed of my Beloved—
He was coming to me in the darkness of night.
The melody of the Man I love awakened me.
I heard his knock at my heart's door
As he pleaded with me:

[The Bridegroom-King]

Arise, my love.
Open your heart, my darling,
Deeper still to me.

a 4:16–5:1 The beautiful bride overflowing with his life is to be given to others, even as Jesus was given to us by the Father. She has become a feast for the nations, wine to cheer the hearts of others.

Will you receive me this dark night?
There is no one else but you,
My friend, my equal.
I need you this night to arise
And come be with me.
You are my pure, loyal dove,
A perfect partner for me.
My flawless one, will you arise?
For my heaviness and tears
Are more than I can bear.
I have spent myself for you
Throughout the dark night.[a]

[The Sleeping Bride]

³I have already laid aside
My own garments for you.
How could I take them up again
Since I've yielded my righteousness to yours?[b]
You have cleansed my life and taken me so far.
Isn't that enough?

a 5:2 The Hebrew text literally means "My head is filled with dew and my hair with the drops of the night." This is clearly a picture of Jesus as the Gethsemane Man, the one who prayed all night for us (John 17). This translation takes the liberty of taking the implicit and making it explicit in order to express the dynamic equivalent and aid the reader in understanding the scene.

b 5:3 Garments in the Bible are frequently used as a picture of righteousness. Filthy garments are a symbol of unrighteousness or self-righteousness. Clean white garments are a picture of the righteousness of Christ. Laying aside her garments is a symbolic picture of what happens when we come to know Jesus as Savior—we lay aside our self-righteousness and take up his garments of true righteousness.

⁴My Beloved reached into me
To unlock my heart.
The core of my very being trembled at his touch.
How my soul melted when he spoke to me!
⁵My spirit arose to open
For more of his touch.
As I surrendered to him,
I began to sense his fragrance—
The fragrance of his suffering love.
It was the scent of myrrh
Flowing all through me.
⁶I opened my soul to my Beloved,
But suddenly he was gone!
My heart was torn out
In longing for him.
I sought his presence, his fragrance,
But could not find him anywhere.
I called out for him,
Yet he did not answer me.
I will arise and search for him
Until I find him.
⁷As I walked throughout the city
In search of him,
The overseers stopped me
As they made their rounds.
They beat me and bruised me
Until I could take no more.

They wounded me deeply
And removed their covering from me.
⁸Nevertheless, make me this promise,
You brides-to-be:
If you find my Beloved One,
Please tell him
I endured all travails for him.
I've been pierced through by love,a
And I will not be turned aside!

[Jerusalem maidens, brides-to-be]

⁹*What love is this?*
How could you continue to care
So deeply for him?
Isn't there another who could
Steal away your heart?
We see now your beauty,
More beautiful than all the others.
What makes your Beloved
Better than any other?
What is it about him
That makes you ask us
To promise you this?

---

a 5:8 As translated from the Septuagint.

[The Shulamite Bride]

[10]He alone is my Beloved.

He shines in dazzling splendor,

Yet is still so approachable—

Without equal as he stands above all others,

Waving his banner to myriads.

[11]The way he leads me is divine.

His leadership—so pure and dignified

As he wears his crown of gold.

Upon this crown are letters of black

Written on a background of glory.[a]

[12]He sees everything with pure understanding.

How beautiful his insights—without distortion.

His eyes rest upon the fullness

Of the river of revelation,

Flowing so clean and pure.

[13]Looking at his gentle face

I see such fullness of emotion.

Like a lovely garden where fragrant spices grow—[b]

What a Man!

No one speaks words so anointed as this one—[c]

---

a 5:11 Many Jewish interpreters have seen the phrase "His locks are black as a raven" as pointing us to the letters of the Law written in heaven. Jewish rabbis teach that the precepts of the Word of God (Torah) are written in the heavenly realm, with black letters on top of white flames of glory fire. (Hebrew letters can appear as locks of hair.)

b 5:13 The Hebrew text is literally "like a tower of fragrance." These beds of spices would picture a garden of emotion and sweetness coming forth from her Beloved.

c 5: 13 See Psalm 45:2, a psalm with an inscription stating it was written to the "tune of lilies."

Words that both pierce and heal,

Words like lilies dripping with myrrh.

¹⁴See how his hands hold unlimited power!

But he never uses it in anger,

For he is always holy, displaying his glory.

His innermost place is a work of art—

So beautiful and bright.

How magnificent and noble is this One—

Covered in majesty!

¹⁵He is steadfast in all he does.

His ways are the ways of righteousness,

Based on truth and holiness.

None can rival him,

But all will be amazed by him.

¹⁶Most sweet are his kisses,

Even his whispers of love.

He is delightful in every way

And perfect from every viewpoint.

If you ask me why I love him so,

O brides-to-be,

It's because there is none like him to me.

Everything about him

Fills me with holy desire!

And now he is my Beloved—

My Friend forever.

Six

[Brides-to-be]

[1]O rarest of beauty,
Where then has your Lover gone?
We long to see him too.
Where may we find him?
We will follow you as you seek after him.

[The Shulamite Bride]

[2]My Lover has gone down
Into his garden of delight,
The place where his spices grow,
To feast with those pure in heart.
I know we shall find him there.
[3]He is within me—I am his garden of delight.
I have him fully and now he fully has me!

[The Bridegroom-King]

⁴O my beloved, you are striking—
Lovely even in your weakness.
When I see you in your beauty,
I see a radiant city,
Where we will dwell as one.ᵃ
More pleasing than any pleasure,
More delightful than any delight,
You have ravished my heart,
Stealing away my strength to resist you.
Even hosts of angels stand in awe of you.ᵇ
⁵Turn your eyes from me;
I can't take it anymore!
I can't resist the passion
Of these eyes that I adore.
Overpowered by a glance,
My ravished heart—undone.
Held captive by your love,
I am truly overcome!ᶜ

---

a 6:4 The text includes a reference to Jerusalem. For the Jew, it is the city where God and man lived together. For the believer, it points us to the New Jerusalem, where God and man dwell in holy union.

b 6:4 This is how various Hebrew scholars have interpreted the phrase "You have captured my heart" or "Awe inspiring, as an army with banners."

c 6:5 The Hebrew word for "overcome" is *Rahab*. Like the harlot who was chosen, favored, saved from Jericho's destruction, and included in the genealogy of Jesus, so you have "overcome" his heart. No one would have thought Rahab would be so honored, and many have said that about you. You have overcome many things, but to overcome him is love's delight.

For your undying devotion to me
Is the most yielded sacrifice.[a]
[6]The shining of your spirit[b]
Shows how you have taken my truth
To become balanced and complete.
[7]Your beautiful blushing cheeks
Reveal how real your passion is for me,
Even hidden behind your veil of humility.
[8]I could have chosen any
From among the vast multitude
Of royal ones who follow me.[c]
[9]But one is my beloved dove—
Unrivaled in your beauty,
Without equal, beyond compare,
The perfect one, the only one for me.
Others see your beauty and sing of your joy.
Brides and queens chant your praise:
"How blessed is she!"
[10]Look at you now—
Arising as the dayspring of the dawn,
Fair as the shining moon.

---

a 6:5 Literally, "Your hair is like a wave of goats streaming down Mount Gilead." We see hair as a picture of our devotion to Christ. See also Song of Songs 4:1.

b 6:6 The word used in most translations is *teeth*, which is taken from a Hebrew root word that some believe means "white" or "shining." With our teeth we chew the Word of God and process its truths.

c 6:8 The Hebrew text literally means "Sixty queens, eighty brides, and endless numbers of women."

Bright and brilliant
As the sun in all its strength.
Astonishing to behold
As a majestic army
Waving banners of victory.

[The Shulamite Bride]

[11]I decided to go down to the valley streams
Where the orchards of the King grow and mature.
I longed to know if hearts were opening.
Are the budding vines blooming with new growth?
Has their springtime of passionate love arrived?
[12]Then suddenly my longings transported me.
My divine desire brought me
Next to my Beloved Prince,
Sitting with him in his royal chariot.
We were lifted up together![a]

[Zion maidens, brides-to-be]

[13]*Come back! Return to us, O maiden of his majesty.*
Dance for us as we gaze upon your beauty.

---

a 6:12 Considered to be the most difficult verse to translate in the Song of Songs, the meaning of the Hebrew is uncertain.

[The Shulamite Bride]

Why would you seek a mere Shulamite like me?
Why would you want to see my dance of love?

[The Bridegroom-King]

Because you dance so gracefully,
As though you danced with angels.[a]

---

a 6:13 This is literally the "dance of Mahanaim" or "the dance of two armies." When Jacob (Israel) returned to the Promised Land, he entered at Mahanaim, the place where two camps of angels gathered. See Genesis 32:1–2.

Seven

---

¹How beautiful on the mountains
Are the sandaled feet of this one
Bringing such good news.
You are truly royalty!
The way you walk so gracefully in my ways
Displays such dignity.
You are truly the poetry of God—
His very handiwork.
²⁻³Out of your innermost being
Is flowing the fullness of my Spirit—
Never failing to satisfy.
Within your womb there is
A birthing of harvest wheat;
They are the sons and daughters nurtured
By the purity you impart.
How gracious you have become!
⁴Your life stands tall as a tower,
Like a shining light on a hill.

Your revelation eyes are pure,
Like pools of refreshing—
Sparkling light for a multitude.
Such discernment surrounds you,
Protecting you from the enemy's advance.
⁵Redeeming love crowns you as royalty.
Your thoughts are full of
Life, wisdom, and virtue.
Even a King is held captive by your beauty.
⁶How delicious your fair beauty;
It cannot be described
As I count the delights you bring to me.
Love has become the greatest.
⁷You stand in victory above the rest,
Stately and secure
As you share with me your vineyard of love.
⁸Now I decree, I will ascend and arise.
I will take hold of you with my power,
Possessing every part of my fruitful bride.
Your love I will drink as wine,
And your words will be mine.
⁹For your kisses of love are exhilarating,
More than any delight
I've known before.
Your kisses of love awaken
Even the lips of sleeping ones
To kiss me as you have done.

[The Shulamite Bride]

[10]Now I know that I am filled with my Beloved
And all his desires are fulfilled in me.
[11]Come away, my Lover.
Come with me to the far away fields.
We will run away together to the forgotten places
And show them redeeming love.
[12]Let us arise and run to the vineyards of your people
And see if the budding vines of love
Are now in full bloom.
We will discover if their passion is awakened.[a]
There I will display my love for you.
[13]The love apples are in bloom,
Sending forth their fragrance of spring.
The rarest of fruits are found at our doors—
The new as well as the old.
I have stored them for you,
My Lover-Friend!

---

a   7:12 Pomegranates are equated to human passion and emotions. When opened, they are a blushing fruit and speak powerfully of our hearts of passion opened to our Lover.

Eight

[1]If only I could show everyone
This passionate desire I have for you.
If only I could express it fully,
No matter who was watching me,
Without shame or embarrassment.
[2]I long to bring you to my innermost chamber—
This holy sanctuary you have formed within me.
O that I might carry you within me.
I would give you the spiced wine of my love,
This full cup of bliss that we share.
We would drink our fill until...
[3]His left hand cradles my head
While his right hand holds me close.
We are at rest in this love.
[4]Promise me, brides-to-be,
By the gentle gazelles and delicate deer,
That you'll not disturb my love
Until he is ready to arise.

[The Bridegroom-King]

⁵Who is this one? Look at her now!
She arises out of her desert,
Clinging to her Beloved.
When I awakened you
Under the apple tree,
As you were feasting upon me,
I awakened your innermost being
With the travail of birth
As you longed for more of me.
⁶Fasten me upon your heart
As a seal of fire forevermore.
This living, consuming flame
Will seal you as my prisoner of love.ᵃ
My love is stronger than the chains
Of death and the grave,
All consuming as the very flashes of fire
From the burning heart of God.
Place this fierce, unrelenting fire
Over your entire being.
⁷Rivers of pain and persecution
Will never extinguish this flame.
Endless floods will be unable
To quench this raging fire

a 8:6 The ancient Hebrew word for "seal" can also be translated "prison cell." He longs for his bride to be his love prisoner, in the prison cell of his eternal love.

That burns within you.
Everything will be consumed.
It will stop at nothing
As you yield everything
To this furious fire
Until it won't even seem to you
Like a sacrifice anymore.

[The Shulamite Bride]

8-10My brothers said to me when I was young,
"Our sister is so immature.
What will we do to guard her
For her wedding day?"

[The Bridegroom-King]

"We will build a tower of redemption
To protect her.
Since she is vulnerable,
We will enclose her
With a wall of cedar boards."

[The Shulamite Bride]

But now I have grown and become a bride,
And my love for him has made me

A tower of passion and
Contentment for my Beloved.
I am now a firm wall of protection for others,
Guarding them from harm.
This is how he sees me—
I am the one who brings him bliss,
Finding favor in his eyes.
[11]My Bridegroom-King has a vineyard of love
Made from a multitude of followers.[a]
His caretakers of this vineyard
Have given my Beloved their best.
[12]But as for my own vineyard of love,
I give it all to you forever.
And I will give double honor
To those who serve my Beloved
And have watched over my soul.
[13]My Beloved, one with me in my garden,
How marvelous
That my friends, the brides-to-be,
Now hear your voice and song.
Let me now hear it again!

a 8:11 The Hebrew text literally means "Solomon had a vineyard at Baal-Hamon." The king's vineyard is a picture of the church, the called-out multitude of those who follow Jesus. Baal-Hamon can be translated "lord of a multitude," "lord of an uproar," or "lord of wealth."

[The Bridegroom and Bride in Divine Duet]

[14]Arise, my darling!
Come quickly, my Beloved.
Come and be the graceful gazelle with me.
Come be like a dancing deer with me.
We will dance in the high place of the sky,
Yes, on the mountains of fragrant spice.
Forever we shall be
United as one!

About the Translator

Dr. Brian Simmons is known as a passionate lover of God. After a dramatic conversion to Christ, Brian knew that God was calling him to go to the unreached people of the world and present the gospel of God's grace to all who would listen. With his wife Candice and their three children, he spent nearly eight years in the tropical rain forest of the Darien Province of Panama as a church planter, translator, and consultant. Brian was involved in the Paya-Kuna New Testament translation project. He studied linguistics and Bible translation principles with New Tribes Mission. After their ministry in the jungle, Brian was instrumental in planting a thriving church in New England (U.S.), and now travels full time as a speaker and Bible teacher. He has been happily married to Candice for over forty-two years and is known to boast regularly of his children and grandchildren. Brian and Candice may be contacted at:

brian@passiontranslation.com

Facebook.com/passiontranslation

Twitter.com/tPtBible

For more information about the translation project or any of Brian's books, please visit:

www.thepassiontranslation.com

www.stairwayministries.org

www.thepassiontranslation.com